THE LEGEND OF THE O.K. CORRAL

To Anna

RIO NUEVO PUBLISHERS®
P.O. Box 5250, Tucson, Arizona 85703-0250
(520) 623-9558, www.rionuevo.com

Text © 2005 by Ed Finn. See page 64 for photo and illustration copyrights. All rights reserved. No part of this book may be reproduced, stored, introduced into a retrieval system, or otherwise copied in any form without the prior written permission of the publisher, except for brief quotations in reviews or citations.

Design: Karen Schober, Seattle, Washington
Front cover illustration © Thom Ross, *Walking to the O.K. Corral,* acrylic on canvas.
Pictured on page 1: detail from photograph on page 19.

Library of Congress Cataloging-in-Publication Data

Finn, Ed, 1980-
 The legend of the O.K. Corral / Ed Finn.
   p. cm. -- (Look West series)
 Includes bibliographical references.
 ISBN-13: 978-1-887896-71-9 (hardcover)
 ISBN-10: 1-887896-71-6 (hardcover)
 1. Earp, Wyatt, 1848-1929. 2. Earp, Morgan, 1851-1882. 3. Holliday, John Henry, 1851-1887. 4. Frontier and pioneer life--Arizona--Tombstone. 5. Outlaws--Arizona--Tombstone--History--19th century. 6. Violence--Arizona--Tombstone--History--19th century. 7. Tombstone (Ariz.)--History--19th century. I. Title. II. Series: Look West.
 F819.T6F56 2005
 979.1'53--dc22

2005004664

Printed in Hong Kong
10 9 8 7 6 5 4 3 2 1

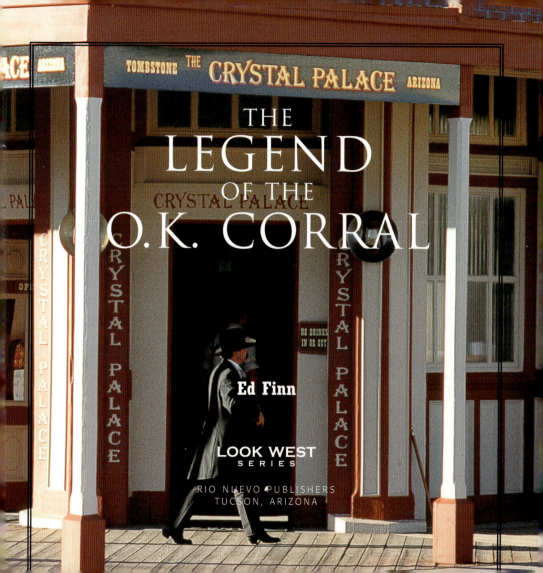

THE LEGEND OF THE O.K. CORRAL

Ed Finn

LOOK WEST SERIES

RIO NUEVO PUBLISHERS
TUCSON, ARIZONA

WYATT EARP'S NUMBER IS BURNING A HOLE IN MY POCKET. BUT WHAT WILL I SAY TO THE MAN WHO EMBODIES SO MUCH HISTORY, SO MANY STORIES OF THE OLD WEST? WHAT WOULD HE TELL ME ABOUT TOMBSTONE, ARIZONA, AND THE GUNFIGHT AT THE O.K. CORRAL? THE HISTORY BOOKS SAY EARP AND HIS BROTHERS TANGLED WITH A GANG OF OUTLAWS, LEAVING THREE MEN DEAD AND A TRAIL OF BLOOD TO COME. BUT WHAT REALLY HAPPENED, AND WHY?

Famous Westerns, old books, and a few minutes in history class created my image of Earp and the battle of Tombstone. As a poet and a writer, I'm a magpie by inclination, always hunting out the shiniest part of any story. So I keep wondering: Who is the original who inspired all those copies?

CALLING UP WYATT

> All the world's a stage,
> And all the men and women, merely players.
> They have their exits and their entrances,
> And one man in his time plays many parts ...
>
> —WILLIAM SHAKESPEARE, *AS YOU LIKE IT*

When I finally do interview him, Wyatt is just the man his admirers describe—well-spoken, polite, charming, even philosophical.

"I guess, if anything, if you've got a name," he says, "you have responsibility not only to honor the name but to have compassion for people in their varied reactions to the name—to be empathetic."

Some of this, surely, is studied, but it's clear that charm runs thick in the Earp blood. Wyatt, you see, is the great-grandnephew of Wyatt Berry Stapp Earp, and an intimate of his ancestor's peculiar history. Not only does this Wyatt look strikingly like his forefather, he plays him frequently in a one-man show written by his wife, Terry Earp. Of course, there are differences—the contemporary Wyatt sells insurance for a living, coaches a swim team, and competes in Ironman competitions. But some things are still the same.

Wyatt Earp the younger.

The name Wyatt Earp still carries weight.

I ask Wyatt what reactions he gets from people when he introduces himself.

"Everything from disbelief, to skepticism, to enthusiasm, to respect," Earp explains. "I cannot be paged in an airport. As a child, initially, all my friends wanted to take out Wyatt Earp, so I learned the benefit of a left jab and a right cross. But soon after, I learned to have a sense of humor about it.

"I have a love of people, even the ones that misbehave. They know not what they do. And Wyatt was that way. He was a humanist. He hit people upside the head because it was more practical. He didn't want to kill people. If he even saw someone abusing an animal, he would whip the tar out of them."

When Earp plays his ancestor onstage, he quotes another mysterious cultural icon. "*As You Like It* was my favorite: 'I earn that I eat, get that I wear, owe no man hate, envy no man's happiness, glad of other men's good, content with my harm.' That Shakespeare—now there was a wise man."

The first Wyatt infused his life with great stories and fine words—his interest in newspapers, theater, and literature culminated in efforts to have his biography presented properly in a book, or better yet, a screenplay. There's something in his roving life across the West, his friendship with the unlikable Doc Holliday, his endless plans, prospects, and programs, that reminds us of our most hopeful selves.

It's obvious that the living Wyatt also feels a deep kinship with his ancestor and enjoys playing him immensely. "If anything, perhaps, it's a thank-you to him to do it. He'd always wanted the story of his life told correctly." That story, as Wyatt performs it, stretches from Monmouth, Illinois, to Nome, Alaska, before settling down to a quiet old age in California.

Who was the original Wyatt Berry Stapp Earp? In his time he played many parts. As a traveler, gambler, lawman, prospector, and businessman, Earp became a minor celebrity wherever he went. Born on March 19, 1848, "he was a man of his times," says modern Wyatt. "It's important to put things in the context and frame of those times."

Wyatt Earp as a young lawman with friend Bat Masterson.

Wyatt was one of five brothers (James, Virgil, Wyatt, Morgan, and Warren) and one half-brother, Newton, the ancestor of today's Wyatt. Films portray him as everything from a spotless knight with a shining badge to an ambivalent gambler. And then there are all the roles Wyatt himself played as the West erupted onto the American stage. He was a part-time lawman, an occasional saloon keeper, a one-time boxing judge, a bounty hunter, and nearly always something of a prospector. The only arena where Wyatt never had any luck (though not for lack of interest) was politics.

However, the centerpiece of Earp's fame is the gunfight at the O.K. Corral. The young town of Tombstone, Arizona Territory, saw years of bad blood boil down to an outburst of gunfire that left three men dead in a day. Later, Wyatt's brother Morgan died in an assassination, while another, Virgil, barely survived. Finally, at least three more men died to avenge them and close out the killings.

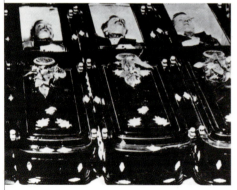

Tom McLaury, Frank McLaury, and Billy Clanton before their burial.

For Wyatt Berry Stapp Earp, however, getting the story right was just as important as the deeds behind it. His modern double embodies that sentiment, living through his ancestor's life on and off the stage.

"Notoriety has been the bane of my life," says the Earp in the play. "My story's been told and untold and retold so many times…."

"It's like being remembered for a car wreck where people were killed," says the modern Wyatt. "For the rest of your life."

Wyatt and Terry Earp offer a couple of haunting details that have come down to them about the gunfight. "There was snow on the ground," he says, "from the day before."

And there was something else: "Children had to take a different way home from school that day so they wouldn't see the blood," adds Terry somberly. "It was like pigs being slaughtered."

To understand Wyatt Earp, and his place at the heart of the historical West, we must explore his stomping grounds. The scrappy town of Tombstone witnessed many dramas, and the silver hills above it lured men and women thousands of miles to seek fame and fortune on its dusty streets. The West was full of such wanderers.

Or as Wyatt put it to me, "What life's all about is the anticipation and the seeking."

Tombstone's first settlers prepared the ground for Wyatt Earp with their frontier fears and dreams. Here is their story.

THE BIRTH OF TOMBSTONE

You soon got into the habit of squinting your eyes, a habit so noticeable in old-timers in looking at the landscape, and, too, you acquire[d] a patience you never knew before—a patience to look calmly at some spot on the horizon … and you resign yourself to the slow shuffle of your cow-pony mount who will tire out if you push him faster.

—JOHN PLESENT GRAY (early southern Arizona rancher, b. 1860), quoted in *And Die in the West: The Story of the O.K. Corral Gunfight*

By 1877, the year Ed Schieffelin started prospecting near Fort Huachuca, the pattern of the mining boomtown was well established. The soldiers at the fort told him he would find nothing but his tombstone in nearby hills full of Apache Indians. Schieffelin persevered, traveling in arroyos to avoid detection and sleeping a half mile from his campfire. He was down to his last 30 cents and dressed in rags before one of his ore samples assayed for nearly $2,000 to the ton.

VOCABULARY

BUFFALO "To intimidate, as by a display of confidence or authority" (*Webster's Dictionary*). In Tombstone: to stun or subdue by hitting upside the head with a pistol butt.

FARO A game in which bets are placed on a pair of cards drawn by a dealer. Each round, the first card is the "loser" and the second is the "winner." Players bet on what numbers the winning and losing cards will have (suits don't count).

HOSTLER One employed to tend horses, especially at a saloon or stable.

KENO A lottery-style betting game in which players bet on balls drawn from a large container.

LEGEND "An unverified story handed down from the past, especially one believed to be historical … a romanticized or popularized myth of modern times." (*American Heritage Dictionary*).

POKER The most popular gambling game of the West, it was played with infinite variations, usually by 2 to 10 players drawing 5 or 7 cards. During several rounds of betting each player "folds" (gives up and loses his bet), "calls" (matches the current bet), or "raises" (increases the current bet).

SAND Guts, courage.

SPECIE Coined money, especially gold and silver.

STAGE A stagecoach was drawn by a team of horses. Wells, Fargo offered coaches with a shotgun guard to protect travelers and valuables sent aboard its lines, and backed it up with full insurance for stolen property.

Other prospectors were hot on his heels, but Fortune smiled on Ed's endeavors: the Apaches moved to Mexico, weathering the assaults of U.S. Army troops, and the prospectors discovered their first big claims, the Lucky Cuss and Tough Nut.

Schieffelin and his partners made their first profits by selling the Contention (so named because it was a source of argument with another prospecting team) for $10,000, or about $175,000 today. That mine produced $5 million of bullion in its first five years; today the same haul would be worth roughly $80 million.

Mining created an insatiable demand for lumber and water in a region that had little of either. The wealth it generated drove equally insatiable needs for saloons, gambling halls, and bordellos. The first buildings in Tombstone went up in 1879; within a year two thousand people lived there, and by 1881 it was the second-largest city in Arizona, after Tucson. On October 2,

Earpiana includes stamps and postmarks.

1879, the first edition of the *Tombstone Nugget* reported with satisfaction: "Strangers are pressing in upon us in great numbers, and building lots are being sold as rapidly as the proper papers can be made out."

Buildings signaled not only the arrival of cash but also of trouble. Explosive population growth, open range, and new army posts full of hungry soldiers combined with the tempting proximity of the Mexican border to make cattle rustling something of a regional sport. While some "cowboys" were just honest ranchers and hired hands, others took advantage of the Arizona free-for-all to expand from cattle herding to cattle raiding, stagecoach robbing, and other lucrative frontier crimes. As Tombstone grew, the term cowboy came to be used as a slur by many, who viewed rowdy, rural gunslingers as criminals by default.

TOMBSTONE TODAY

It is a place more pretentious than I had imagined, and full of activity, notwithstanding the hundreds of loungers seen upon the streets. The only attractive places visible are the liquor and gambling saloons, which are everywhere present and are carpeted and comfortable furnished.

—CLARA SPALDING BROWN, *San Diego Tribune,* July 7, 1880

In some ways, Tombstone hasn't changed much since then. Now the prized commodity is tourism, not silver or lumber.

Most visitors' first taste of the town is Boot Hill, a graveyard whose fame increased as it added more notorious victims and killers

Tombstone revelers in period costume.

to its roster. Perched above a spectacular vista of the San Pedro Valley, the site offers Tombstone in a nutshell: fascinating, tumultuous history and the clamor of tourism set in the austere beauty of the southern Arizona desert.

The town's few square blocks of prime real estate unfold in a mix of dust and shimmering air above baking asphalt. Citizen actors patrol the streets in elaborate period costumes, flourishing everything from lace frills and bustles to top hats and shotguns. At every corner bands of lawmen or cowboys are gathering for the gunfight. And commence it does, several times a day like clockwork, as various saloons and show groups sponsor their own variations on the famous shoot-out near the O.K. Corral.

For all its showmanship and bustle, Tombstone has a few sanctuaries, too: saloons emblazoned with advertising also offer air conditioning and lunch. Many of them provided settings for famous quarrels, dalliances, and murders. The Tombstone Courthouse State Historic Park museum, the Tombstone Western Heritage Museum, and the Rose Tree Museum, home to the "World's Largest Rose Bush," house many fascinating objects, including weapons and documents from Wyatt Earp's era.

THE TOMBSTONE SCENE, 1880

As the silver business boomed, newly wealthy Tombstone quickly expanded. Not one but two newspapers, the *Nugget* and the *Epitaph*, sprang up. Stately hotels materialized as if conjured by a silvery genie, offering decadent pleasures in sumptuous dining rooms: the Crystal Palace, the Oriental, the Grand Hotel….

Revelers could take in Shakespeare or Gilbert and Sullivan at Schieffelin Hall, and more urbane performances at the Bird Cage. A reporter from Chicago, A. H. Noon, grumbled: "The atmosphere is dirty and abominable, but they dance away nevertheless—the men inanely grinning, the women evidently dancing as a matter of business." Drinking tended to run into fighting as the evenings drew on. Later, renovators of the Bird Cage found 150 bullet holes in its weathered walls.

Fancy restaurants lured diners with European wines, oysters from San Francisco, ice cream, and other luxuries, though fruits and vegetables were still hard to come by. In the saloons, bartenders served out whiskey and hard liquor, home-brewed beer, champagne, and mixed drinks ranging from mint juleps to the Champagne Flip, which combined a raw egg with a dash of sugar in bubbly. Some regular customers were good for $20 or $25 a day at the bar, or about $400 in today's dollars.

Unsurprisingly, a popular saloon could pay just as well as hunting the silver yourself. One Arizonan, a man named F. Bennet, borrowed $500 to purchase an established saloon: "Well do you know there was six weeks I never saw a bed; just slept on the billiard tables; I kept right by the saloon and never closed it night or day. I made $20,000."

Tombstone's silver proved an irresistible draw for thousands.

Tombstone catered to every reckless pleasure, from prostitution to opium dens. "Soiled doves" found easy work in the rollicking saloons and gambling dens, and may even have been officially licensed by Tombstone authorities. The tumultuous atmosphere made social relationships more ambiguous. Jim Earp's wife, Bessie, was arrested for running a brothel in Wichita, Kansas, and there is some evidence Mattie and Sadie, two of Wyatt's three wives, may have engaged in prostitution.

GAMES OF CHANCE

The big money, however, was in gambling. For professional gamblers, men loaded down with silver nuggets and weekly wages proved easy targets. Miners would liquor up and complacently gamble their earnings away. "Far from manifesting any great regret over the loss," recalled one old-timer, they seemed "buoyed up by a sense of duty performed."

Consequently, a second wave of fortune-seekers followed the silver-hunting pioneers. As the *Tombstone Epitaph* reported in 1880, "The Call of 'Free Roll' at the keno game, will collect a bigger crowd in 10 minutes than the cry of 'fire' on a windy night." The big games on the frontier were keno, faro, and poker, all card games that rewarded close study, but rewarded the house purse even more.

THE CITIZENS

News of Tombstone's mineral wealth spread quickly throughout the U.S. The national economy was in a slump, which encouraged even well-established citizens—stockbrokers, doctors, investors—to seek out easy money in the Wild West. So who were these men and women of Tombstone?

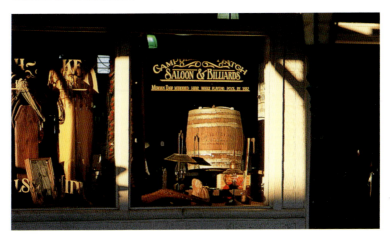

Saloons were the best business in town.

Opinions differed. One depressed Wells, Fargo employee wrote back to his fiancée: "Tombstone has a population of six thousand—five thousand of them are bad—one thousand of them known outlaws. I don't want much of Tombstone." These were the gamblers and drinkers who populated the town's cheery dens of vice.

But every stratum of American society was represented, from bottom to top. The highbrow element held the exclusive Martha Washington Tea Party annually in Schieffelin Hall, where a minuet was danced as part of the entertainment. These "respectable citizens" were careful not to mix excessively with the hoi polloi. They respected the work of lawmen like the Earps, but there were limits: When Virgil Earp applied for membership in the Masonic Lodge, he was rejected.

Other levels of society, however, proved more fluid. George Parsons, a former bank teller from San Francisco, lamented the lax morality of the West: "How men of good family and connections east can come here and marry prostitutes—take them out of a dance hall—I can't see." This

Lawmen gather for a costumed showdown.

criticism could easily be applied to the Earps—although of the four brothers in Tombstone, only Jim was legally married.

The rough and tumble of Tombstone attracted a wide variety of characters. Mayor John Clum left his father's farm in New York for the army, eventually becoming a federal Indian agent and then a newspaper editor. "Big Nose" Kate, Doc Holliday's sometime companion, was the Hungarian daughter of the Emperor Maximilian's personal surgeon. Jim Smith, a hostler, was a black Civil War vet who later earned Tombstone's respect for staring down Buckskin Frank Leslie, a character who once shot a man down without losing the light on his cigarette. Aside from the gunslingers, Tombstone also was home to hundreds of peaceable business people, including immigrants from Europe, Mexico, and China.

THE FIGHTING PREACHER

Talk about muscular Christianity. We overheard a miner yesterday say, upon having the Episcopal minister pointed out to him, "Well, if that lad's argument was a hammer, and religion a drill, he'd knock a hole in the hanging wall of skepticism."

—*Tombstone Nugget,* February 18, 1882

One of the Tombstone characters who proved most adept at straddling the many divisions in town society was Endicott Peabody, a twenty-five-year-old seminarian who arrived on the stagecoach in January of 1882. His mission was to raise enough money to build the Arizona Territory's first Episcopal church, and he wasted no chance to complete it.

"He's a sensible, manly fellow ... quite an athlete and of magnificent build, weighing two hundred pounds, muscles hard as iron," reported George Parsons. An avid boxer, Peabody won the miners over by defeating their champion, and he earned the respect of the cowboys by staring down any who dared interrupt his church services. On at least two occasions, Peabody raised money directly from gambling tables, and he would often visit saloons in the evening, encouraging revelers to hear his upcoming sermons.

COWBOYS AND INDIANS

Come to think of it, it takes some sand to drive a stage through that kind of country, with thousands of dollars in the front boot and the chance of a Winchester behind every rock.

—WYATT EARP, *San Francisco Examiner*, August 9, 1896

Tombstone's manic economy was predicated on great reward, but every citizen risked his or her life to work there. While much was made of the town's sensational dangers—highwaymen and Apaches—Tombstone residents were more likely to die from disease or in a drunken fight.

The town's increasing wealth made it a prime venue for robbers, and the Wells, Fargo stagecoach was the perfect target. Because Wells, Fargo insured all customers against theft, mines and individuals would complacently send thousands of dollars in coin and silver out of Tombstone by coach. It was just such a robbery that started the events leading to the gunfight at the O.K. Corral.

CAST OF CHARACTERS

Even before the gunfight, several of the participants were famous in Arizona. And when newspapers hit the streets across the U.S. the next morning, all of them became notorious.

THE EARP PARTY

Jimmy, as he is familiarly called, is one of the jolliest, best-natured men that ever the sun shone on.... Bacchus would occasionally get the better of him, but Jimmy never hunted fights, and if he accidentally found one would, as soon as sober, fix things up. Virgil was of different texture. Marshal of Tombstone for months, he kept the town quiet as a cemetery. Poor Morgan was as brave and reckless a man as ever put foot in stirrup or pulled the trigger on a 45. Wyatt, who never drank, was as cool as the icebergs in Alaska, brave and determined as any man on earth, and General of the whole outfit.

—*San Francisco Examiner,* May 11, 1882

James Earp *June 28, 1841–January 25, 1926*

James was the eldest of the Earp brothers in Tombstone. Injured in the Civil War, he kept himself out of his younger brothers' scrapes and law enforcement. Instead, his genial personality made him a well-liked bartender. He did not participate in the gunfight at the O.K. Corral.

Virgil Earp *July 18, 1843–October 19, 1905*

Virgil Earp also fought for the Union Army in the Civil War, as did his half-brother, Newton. After the war, he drove stages, worked as a night watchman, and was a constable in Prescott, Arizona. In

Tombstone he worked as a deputy U.S. Marshal—a low-paying position supporting local law enforcement. He was also Tombstone's City Marshall, or chief of police. Six feet tall with piercing blue eyes, Virgil was the most respectable of the Earps, but also the most hot-headed. He wasn't the world's best shot. According to an *Epitaph* story from November 21, 1880, he and Doc Holliday entered a shooting contest with twelve others. Virgil finished fourth. Doc Holliday finished tenth.

Wyatt Earp *March 19, 1848–January 13, 1929*

As a teetotaler, Wyatt Earp was a wild eccentric for the West. He did, however, enjoy ice cream, and frequented Tombstone's ice cream parlors almost daily. Over the course of his storied career, he had three wives, worked in the stagecoach business and as a hunter, and had several stints as a lawman. He may also have engaged in some petty thievery as a young man, and he certainly loved Lady Luck. "You couldn't hardly get him to split any firewood, he was that careful of them long slender hands of his," said Virgil's wife, Allie. "He was always kneadin' his knuckles and shufflin' cards to keep his hands in shape for gamblin'."

Morgan Earp ⚜ *April 24, 1851–March 18, 1882*

Morgan was one of the most charming Earp brothers, though he shared Virgil's temper. He briefly served as a peace officer in Dodge City, Kansas. In Tombstone he rode shotgun for stagecoaches, dealt faro at the Oriental Saloon, refined his pool game, and was involved in the Earp clan's numerous business ventures.

Warren Earp ⚜ *March 9, 1855–July 6, 1900*

Warren wasn't in Tombstone for the gunfight at the OK Corral, but he arrived soon afterward. A formidable fighter, he died nine years later on the floor of a saloon in nearby Willcox, shot dead by an enemy during an argument.

Doc Holliday ⚜ *March 11, 1819–November 8, 1877*

Doc Holliday was one of the most infamous characters in the West. A dentist raised in pre-war Georgia and trained in Philadelphia, Holliday moved to Dallas as a young man to practice his trade. There he was diagnosed with consumption—tuberculosis—and started bringing new meaning to the expression "devil-may-care." "As quarrelsome a man as God ever allowed to live on this earth," according to the *San*

Francisco Examiner, Holliday gambled, drank, and insulted his way into many confrontations, and he was never afraid to draw his guns.

THE CLANTON-McLAURY PARTY

Johnny Behan *October 25, 1845–June 7, 1912*

Behan was good company, the type of man who would always brighten a dinner party as long as he didn't bed the host's wife.

—Casey Tefertiller, *Wyatt Earp: The Life Behind the Legend,* 1997

A former territorial legislator and sheriff, Behan was a charmer hoping to win a political appointment in Cochise, the new Arizona county containing Tombstone. Meanwhile he worked the bar at the Grand Hotel and went in as a partner in a livery stable. By the time of the gunfight he'd gotten his wish, working as sheriff for the new Cochise County. When the bullets started flying, Johnny was watching from the sidelines.

Ike Clanton *1847–June 1887*

Third son of Newman Haynes "Old Man" Clanton, Joseph Isaac Clanton reached Arizona Territory with the rest of his family in the mid 1870s. Their ranch south of Tombstone acted as a clearing-house for rustled cattle, though they probably engaged in legitimate businesses as well. Ike was a lean man with a silly goatee, and the *Tucson Star* once described him and a brother as "wiry, determined-looking men, without a pound of surplus flesh."

Billy Clanton ⚜ *1862–October 26, 1881*

Billy, youngest and tallest of the Clanton boys, was generally considered the best-liked of the bunch. What he lacked in years he made up for in courage, or bold-faced daring: shortly after Wyatt Earp arrived in Tombstone, Billy Clanton stole his horse. When Wyatt confronted him, "he gave the horse up without any service of papers and asked me if I had any more horses to lose," according to transcripts of Wyatt's testimony after the gunfight. "I told him I would keep them in the stable after this and give him no chance to steal them."

Frank McLaury (*March 3, 1848–October 26, 1881*)

The McLaury brothers' ranches may have sheltered cattle stolen by rustlers. Frank, however, contended fiercely that he was an upstanding rancher, once even buying a newspaper ad to defend himself: "My name is well known in Arizona, and thank God this is the first time in my life that the name of dishonesty was ever attached to me."

Tom McLaury *June 30, 1853–26 October 26, 1881*

Along with his brother, Tom McLaury was suspected by many of selling "hot" cattle. However, they did have their defenders. As one contemporary wrote: "These boys were plain, good-hearted, industrious fellows. They may have harbored passing rustlers at their ranch, but what rancher did not? And it would have been little of a man who would have turned away any traveler in that land of long trails and hard going."

THE GUNFIGHT

Cowboys should be declared outlaws ... we hope that the Tombstone Vigilance Committee will act promptly and do their work effectively. It will not be hard work; the rope for a few ringleaders, and the rest of the cowards will thereafter give the place a wide berth.

—*San Francisco Exchange,* March 17, 1881

The men involved in the gunfight near the O.K. Corral, like most killers, did not have simple reasons to go into battle. Conflicting politics mingled with personal rivalries, wounded honor, and greed as they walked towards firing lines just feet apart.

THE BACK STORY

Ike Clanton had been quarreling with the Earp brothers and Doc Holliday for months over an attempted Wells, Fargo stagecoach robbery on March 15, 1881. Two men died as a result of the failed holdup, and despite a grueling manhunt, no culprits had been found. To hear the Earps tell it, Clanton and his associates knew the robbers as fellow cowboys. So Wyatt tried to strike a deal with the Clantons and McLaurys to lure the three culprits back to Tombstone. The cowboys would double-cross their friends, giving the Earps the glory and keeping the reward money for themselves.

Of course, the Clanton gang had a different story. They contended that the Earps wanted the three outlaws killed. According to this version, the Earps, who sometimes worked for Wells, Fargo, had tipped off the robbers that a large shipment of specie was on the coach that night. Worse, it was Wyatt's friend, Doc Holliday, who, according to the Clantons, killed the driver. If the three outlaws could be shot dead, the Clantons would get their reward as hush-up money and the Earps' reputation would be safe.

Complicating the issue, Tombstone's county sheriff, Johnny Behan, maintained ties with both parties, but he too had a feud brewing with Wyatt Earp. Behan had promised but never given Earp a job as under-sheriff and also never paid the Earps for hunting the three stagecoach robbers. But the most painful divide was a personal one. By the fall of 1881, Behan's consort, Josephine Sarah "Sadie" Marcus, was more likely to be seen on the arm of Wyatt Earp than that of Johnny Behan.

THE NIGHT BEFORE

The bad blood between the Earps and the Clantons was getting worse. Worried, Morgan Earp traveled to Tucson to retrieve Doc Holliday from its gambling halls.

On the evening of Tuesday, October 25, 1881, Doc Holliday ran into Ike Clanton at the Alhambra Saloon and confronted him as Virgil, Morgan, and Wyatt Earp looked on. As the argument raged, Virgil turned casually to Morgan: "You're an officer—you should do something about that." Morgan led Holliday outside, where the confrontation continued until Virgil broke it up. Ike vowed to settle the issue "man-to-man" the next day, Morgan headed home, and the others dispersed into several saloons.

What followed was one of the most mystifying displays of civility ever to grace Tombstone's gambling dens. Soon after the confrontation, Ike Clanton, Tom McLaury, Virgil Earp, Johnny Behan, and an unknown player sat down for a game of poker that stretched until 7 a.m. Within hours, two of these men would be shot, one killed, and the character of Tombstone changed forever. What they spoke about, we don't know, but as Virgil left, Ike asked him to carry a message to Doc Holliday: "The damned son of a bitch has got to fight." Virgil refused, and Ike roped him in, too: "You may have to fight before you know it." Paying little heed, Virgil crawled home to bed.

THE NEXT MORNING

It was a cold, windy dawn in Tombstone. But Ike didn't feel the chill, traveling from saloon to saloon and informing all that soon "the ball will open." People kept waking Wyatt and Virgil to tell them of Clanton's threats, but they just went back to sleep. Ike went to Fly's boardinghouse, where Doc Holliday was staying with his companion, Big Nose Kate.

Taking Ike's challenge seriously where the Earps did not, Holliday rose to dress himself. At about the same time, Wyatt and Virgil roused themselves, and around noon Virgil spotted Ike walking down the street ahead of him, sporting a pistol and rifle. Walking up behind him, Virgil buffaloed him with the heel of his pistol, and Clanton crumpled to the ground. With Morgan's help, Virgil dragged his prize to the town's courthouse, where a fight nearly erupted as the Earps and Clanton taunted one another while Virgil searched for a judge.

According to Tombstone law, only police officers could carry guns within the town. Upon entering Tombstone, visitors were to deposit their firearms at the first place they stopped—typically a stable or saloon. The judge fined Ike $25 for breaking this law, and a friend led him off to have a doctor attend his bleeding head. Wyatt walked out of the courthouse and encountered Tom McLaury, whom he proceeded to buffalo several times with his gun.

Meanwhile, Billy Clanton and Frank McLaury had congregated in George Spangenberg's gun shop with Tom McLaury, loading up on ammunition, where Wyatt observed them closely. Ike Clanton joined them and tried to purchase a new pistol, but Spangenberg refused. At the same time, Virgil collected a rifle from the Wells, Fargo office and hurried to meet his brother.

ABOUT 3 P.M.

> The inmates of every house in town were greatly startled by the sudden report of fire arms, about 3 p.m., discharged with such lightening-like rapidity that it could only be compared to the explosion of a bunch of fire-crackers.
>
> —Clara Brown, *San Diego Union*, November 3, 1881

As the two parties moved through the streets of Tombstone, rumors flew fast and thick. Control of the situation suddenly came down to Sheriff Johnny Behan, who had risen late and was getting a shave when he heard about the impending fight. Meeting the Clanton-McLaury group first, he steered them into an empty lot beside Fly's boardinghouse. Behan said he patted Ike Clanton down for weapons, finding none, and tried to persuade the others to hand over their guns. They refused, insisting that they were about to leave town, and Behan agreed to ask the Earps to disarm first.

As Behan approached the Earp party, they were already marching towards Fly's. Doc Holliday carried the Wells, Fargo shotgun and a nickel-plated pistol in a scabbard; Morgan and Wyatt had their six-shooters, and Virgil carried Doc's cane in one hand and his own pistol tucked into his pants. According to the Earps, Behan told them he had disarmed the Clanton gang. But Behan later claimed he said: "I was there for the purpose of arresting and disarming them."

Whatever the truth, Behan was too late to stop the fight. The Earps found the vacant lot behind the O.K. Corral unusually busy. There stood the two McLaurys, Frank and Tom, with their horses, and two Clantons, Billy and Ike, all looking rather grim. Billy Clanton and Frank McLaury kept their hands on their pistols while Tom reached for a rifle on his horse's saddle.

"Throw up your hands," Virgil yelled.

Two shots rang out in rapid succession, followed by a brief pause. Then, just as suddenly, the firing was general. Nobody can agree on who fired those first two shots. Wyatt and Doc Holliday? Wyatt and Billy Clanton? In the ensuing melee, it hardly mattered.

Ike Clanton approached Wyatt and reached out his arms. Wyatt saw that he was unarmed and found himself grappling with Clanton while the shooting continued.

"Go to fighting or get away!" Wyatt yelled to Ike as he shoved him aside. Clanton fled the scene rapidly, later claiming that several bullets nearly found him through the woodwork of nearby buildings.

Frank McLaury was hit almost immediately, though he kept firing. His brother Tom couldn't manage to pull a rifle off his horse as the animal reared in terror at the gunshots. Holliday followed Tom, releasing a charge of buckshot into his chest. Soon Frank tried a similar move, hiding behind his horse and moving towards Fremont Street. Holliday cornered him as well, taking a grazing shot on the hip as he shot Frank in the stomach.

Young Billy Clanton fought resolutely despite several wounds, including one to his wrist. Moving the gun to his other hand, the young Clanton fought on in a pool of his own blood as he gradually sank to earth. When the fighting stopped, he was fumbling to reload, but the photographer Camillus Fly came out and wrested his gun away.

Twenty or thirty seconds after the first *click* of a gun barrel, the street was silent, obscured by a haze of dust and gun smoke. The

McLaurys lay dying on Fremont Street. Virgil was hit in his calf, and a bullet had traveled diagonally through Morgan from one shoulder to the other, chipping his spine. Wyatt remained untouched.

AFTERMATH

A stranger viewing the funeral cortege, which was the largest ever seen in Tombstone, would have thought that some person esteemed by the entire camp was being conveyed to his final resting place ... such a public manifestation of sympathy from so large a portion of the residents of the camp seemed reprehensible when it is remembered that the deceased were nothing more or less than thieves.

—Clara Brown, *San Diego Union*, November 3, 1881

The aftermath of the gunfight got even uglier than the fight itself. Two days after the killings, hundreds turned out to walk the bodies of Billy Clanton, Tom McLaury, and Frank McLaury to their final resting place on Boot Hill, where they were buried in high style. They had been displayed in the undertaker's window with the sign "MURDERED IN THE STREETS OF TOMBSTONE."

The feud between the Earps and Clantons grew more infamous as each revenge killing earned headlines in the following months. "THREE MEN HURLED INTO ETERNITY IN THE DURATION OF A MOMENT," blared the next day's *Epitaph*, while the *Nugget* story declared: "The 26th of October, 1881, will always be marked as one of the crimson days in the annals of Tombstone, a day when blood flowed as water, and human life was held as a shuttlecock."

Almost immediately, the town grew mesmerized by the coroner's inquest as the authorities tried to determine whether the gunfight was murder, self-defense, vigilante justice, or some combination thereof. Officially, the inquest was only supposed to decide whether there was enough evidence to try the Earp party, but it ended up being almost a full-blown trial itself, with each side calling numerous witnesses.

The Tombstone papers printed full transcripts of each day's testimony. As more details about the feud came out, it became increasingly clear that this fight was about more than an attempted stagecoach robbery. The heightened drama of a courtroom battle widened the rifts between the Earps, the Clantons, and those who would rather be rid of both.

‖ VENGEANCE, VENDETTA ‖

The common enemy to us law-abiding citizens and to our Mexican neighbors must be wiped out, root and branch. They should be hunted down like reptiles, and made to pay the penalty of their crimes, without the law's delay.

> —*Arizona Weekly Star,* June 23, 1881
> (weekly edition of *Arizona Daily Star*)

The gunfight at the O.K. Corral, bloody as it was, was not enough to satisfy the two factions. Death threats, lamentations, and accusations continued to fly through Tombstone's streets and newspapers. Then, on December 28, 1882, shotgun blasts shattered the night air, ripping buckshot through Virgil Earp and narrowly missing bystanders in a nearby saloon. Virgil survived the attack but lost much of the use of his right arm and was considered very lucky to survive. "Never mind, I've got one arm left to hug you with," he told his wife as she helped with his wounds.

Wyatt Earp sent a telegram to U.S. Marshal Crawley Dake in Phoenix: "Virgil was shot by concealed assassins last night. His wounds are fatal. Telegraph me appointment with power to appoint deputies. Local authorities are doing nothing. The lives of other citizens are threatened." Dake responded with alacrity: Wyatt now had federal backing to take the fight into his own hands.

Ultimately Ike Clanton was brought to trial for the attempted assassination of Virgil Earp. His hat was found at the scene of the shooting, but in the end this was not enough to convict him. Wyatt later claimed the judge on the case told him: "Wyatt, you'll never clean up this crowd this way; next time you'd better leave your prisoners out in the brush where alibis don't count."

By this point, Wyatt spent most of his time on patrol outside Tombstone, looking for cowboys. He was in town on the night of March 18, however, when Morgan Earp was gunned down through a window as he played pool at Bob Hatch's saloon. Morgan died within the hour, surrounded by the other Earp brothers and their wives.

After sending Morgan's body to his wife and family, Wyatt accompanied the wounded Virgil and his wife, Allie, out of Arizona and received a tip-off that cowboys were waiting for them at the train depot in Tucson. Sure enough, Wyatt saw Ike Clanton hiding on a flatbed car with Frank Stillwell, a deputy to John Behan and friend of the Clantons. These were the two men Wyatt suspected of shooting Virgil and Morgan. Wyatt and some of his posse, including Doc Holliday and Warren Earp, killed Frank Stillwell as he ran. Fleet-footed Ike Clanton escaped once again.

Now the vendetta commenced. The next man to die, Florentino "Indian Charlie" Cruz, may have helped kill Morgan Earp. Meanwhile, Wells, Fargo executives gave the *San Francisco Examiner* an unusual interview, wholeheartedly endorsing Wyatt, their former employee, and even vouching for Doc: "Doc Holliday, although a man of dissipated habits and a gambler, has never been a thief and was never in any way connected with the stage robbery."

Soon after Cruz's death, the Earp posse found itself in an ambush. Wyatt's compatriots turned their horses and fled, but Wyatt faced the enemy. He emptied both barrels into a generally reviled outlaw with links to the Clantons, Curley Bill Brocius, and then drew a pistol to wound another cowboy. Picking up a fallen comrade whose horse had been shot dead, Wyatt regrouped with the rest of the posse. His coat had been shot to tatters, but once again Wyatt was untouched. "Our escape was miraculous," Holliday reported.

There the vendetta ended, though the rumors of gun battles and secret posses would persist for months. The Earp posse faded quietly away despite the efforts of reporters who attempted to track their movements.

‖ REVISIONS ‖

> I have described this battle with as much particularity as possible, partly because there are not many city dwellers who have more than a vague idea of what such a fight really means, and partly because I was rather curious how it would look in cold type.
>
> —Wyatt Earp, *San Francisco Examiner,* August 2, 1896

The facts of the shoot-out were relatively clear. Eight men went in, six were shot, three died. But the issues that led to violence ran deep and murky. The Clantons-McLaurys and the Earps represented two very different elements in the bustling new arena of Arizona Territory. The cowboys, as they came to be called, were country men, a blend of cattle rustlers and ranchers who made a living off the moral ambiguities of the frontier.

When the cowboys came to town after long weeks on the trail, they were ready for some rowdy celebration. The boomtowns were only too ready to service their every need and fleece them for every penny they had. The Earps and Doc Holliday represented the urban half of the equation, the men who operated in a universe of saloons, hotels, casinos, and brothels, roving between the constellations of a few bright city blocks that spangled the vastness of the West.

For men like Wyatt Earp, the life of restless travel between cow towns and silver towns, gold rushes and land grabs, required a certain personal complexity. Historians seeking new angles on his story have cast him in all sorts of ways, from reckless gambler to beloved family man to ruthless enforcer. There's a bit of truth to all of those descriptions, if only because life in a complicated town like Tombstone required everyone to wear many hats—prospector, saloon-keeper, gambler, shotgun messenger, lawman, ladies' man, and entrepreneur, to name a few. Wyatt was all of those things, and more.

The Earps' enmity for the cowboys ran deep because they were hustlers from two different worlds. Because the wealthy new town had so many plum government jobs for the plucking, the split quickly became political as well as personal. The cowboys, frequently Southern and thoroughly rural, were largely Democrats. The new urbanites, Wyatt Earp included, were Republicans. Politics struck quite a nerve for most Americans in the 1880s, only fifteen years after the end of the Civil War.

This political conflict played itself out in the press. The *Tombstone Epitaph* was founded and run by John Clum, who also happened to be Tombstone's mayor. This Republican paper fiercely supported the Earps against their enemies. One Tombstone resident would later recall that to Clum "just about any farmer who was from the South who happened to be a Democrat was automatically a 'cowboy.'"

The *Epitaph* was fought tooth and nail by Harry Woods, deputy sheriff and editor of the Democratic *Tombstone Nugget,* which sided with Sheriff Behan and took a harsh line against the Earps. "I found two daily newspapers published in the city taking sides with the deputy marshal and the sheriff, respectively. Each paper backing its civil clique and berating the other," wrote the territory's acting governor John Gosper to U.S. Secretary of State James Blaine.

Even individual observers found themselves conflicted on the subject. In two letters Endicott Peabody sent home to New England soon after Morgan's murder, the Earp brothers and Tombstone earned equal doses of sympathy and calumny.

To Fannie Peabody, March 20, 1882

We had an excitement on Saturday night—One of the Earps, a family conspicuous for their fighting qualities, was shot in the back while playing billiards in a saloon in the main street. The poor fellow was not killed immediately and suffered frightfully but never uttered a groan. His last sentence was "Well Jim, that's the last game I shall ever play." Fancy a man saying such a thing at such a time. It may show a certain daring but it argues a sad want of any kind of religious feeling or wedded human feeling for his wife and family are in California.

To Julius W. Atwood, March 24, 1882

The feud that I mentioned in my first letter has broken out again—murder & revenge have taken place in quick succession & the town is unrestful-feeling that the end will not come until one of the two factions is entirely annihilated or leaves the country—until that occurs we cannot have a town which will attract capitalists or families. It is a great pity and indeed a very terrible thing that blood should be shed in such a way— the authorities might have suppressed it had they been upright but they are more corrupt than in any place I ever knew and I think only how they may steal the public money & make way with it in riotous living.

A HOUSE OF CARDS

So when those eight men faced each other on October 26, 1881, political disputes had mingled with personal honor. But was it worth dying for? Just a few hours beforehand, Ike Clanton was playing poker with Virgil Earp and Johnny Behan. Surely these men wouldn't have sat around that table for so long if they thought they would be shooting each other the next day? More likely, it was a last-ditch effort to keep things rational, to leave their disagreements behind in a friendly game of poker. It worked, for a while, but a whiskey dawn drove contentment from Ike Clanton's head.

During the trial, the Earps insisted that they only meant to disarm the Clanton gang and run them out of town. The Clantons and McLaurys maintained that's what they wanted, too—they had some of their horses already, they were trying to leave. Perhaps if Behan had been more forceful, or if his top-gun deputies hadn't been out of town chasing criminals, that's exactly what would have happened.

After all, Wyatt had been in several similar situations, staring down armed men, and he almost always managed to end the standoff without a shot fired. One of the great boons of the West was the possibility of melting away into the desert—a man with too many debts could always take a new name in another boomtown, leaving his troubles behind. So while nobody doubted the determination of the Earp or Clanton groups, or their willingness to kill if necessary, there was a sense of shock in Tombstone after the gunfight. In some ways, this was a game of chicken gone wrong.

WYATT EARP, MAN AND LEGEND

You die first, get it? Your friends might get me in a rush, but not before I make your head into a canoe, you understand me?

—Wyatt Earp, played by Kurt Russell in *Tombstone*, 1993

Wyatt took the law into his own hands and hunted down his brother's killers. In the process he inspired a legend. Thanks to the railroad and the telegraph, the story took on immediacy for a nation already fascinated by the rough and tumble world of the Wild West. Dispatches from Tombstone grabbed headlines from San Francisco to New York, often garbling names and details. Descriptions of the incident ranged from "battle" to "street fight," while the *Arizona Daily Star* called it a "sanguinary shooting affray." Farther afield, the *New York Times* told its readers about the gunfight in a brief item under "Criminals and Their Deeds"—and identified the nefarious Doc Holliday as "City Judge Halliday." A New Hampshire local paper said it all happened in the town of "Madstone." The Earp vendetta became a symbol of rough justice in the lawless West.

The story as we know it comes down to us from these news reports, testimony from contemporaries, and later amalgamations of research and interviews. Wyatt himself produced several versions of the story, maneuvering facts to suit his nature or his aging memories. Controversy surrounded the gunfight even in its own day, with each faction supported by its own newspaper and partial witnesses, leaving hardly an unbiased eye to rely on.

Fortunately, Wyatt was his own best press manager. According to Allie Earp, "Wyatt was a crank on reading newspapers. Besides the *Epitaph* and *Nugget* in Tombstone, he took five other papers regular.… If his name was mentioned, he felt better. If it wasn't he was more cranky than ever."

Wyatt never lost his interest in publicity and devoted serious energy towards creating an authoritative version of his life in print. At the same time, he joined the millions of Americans enchanted by moving pictures, and started working on a story intended for the silver screen.

LAWMAN TO THE STARS

Along the way he befriended several sympathetic fellow storytellers, the stars of California's nascent movie business. One day in 1915, Wyatt strolled onto a Hollywood set with Jack London, whom he'd befriended in Alaska. On the set they met director Raoul Walsh and Charlie Chaplin. "When I introduced my guests, [Chaplin] viewed Earp with evident awe. 'You're the bloke from Arizona, aren't you? Tamed the baddies, huh?'" reported Walsh in his memoirs, *Each Man in His Time.*

Wyatt also grew close to some of Hollywood's own famed sheriffs and marshals, including Tom Mix, the young John Wayne, and William S. Hart, probably the most famous screen cowboy of his day. In a letter Wyatt asked Hart's advice: "I realize that I am not going to live to the age of Methuselah, and any wrong impression, I want made right before I go away." Hart's suggestion was to write a book and then turn that into a screenplay.

‖ CELLULOID GUNSLINGERS ‖

Law and Order, 1932, starring Walter Huston, directed by Edward Cahn

Frontier Marshal, 1934, starring George O'Brien, directed by Lewis Seiler

Frontier Marshal, 1939, starring Randolph Scott, directed by Allan Dwan

Dodge City, 1939, starring Errol Flynn, directed by Michael Curtiz

Tombstone, the Town Too Tough to Die, 1942, starring Richard Dix, directed by William McGann

My Darling Clementine, 1946 starring Henry Fonda, directed by John Ford

Law and Order, 1953, starring Ronald Reagan, directed by Nathan Juran

Wichita, 1955, starring Joel McCrea, directed by Jacques Tourneur

Gunfight at the O.K. Corral, 1957, starring Burt Lancaster and Kirk Douglas, directed by John Sturges

Cheyenne Autumn, 1964, starring Richard Widmark, directed by John Ford

Hour of the Gun, 1967, starring James Garner, directed by John Sturges

Doc, 1971, starring Stacy Keach, directed by Frank Perry

Tombstone, 1993, starring Kurt Russell and Val Kilmer, directed by George Cosmatos

Wyatt Earp, 1994, starring Kevin Costner and Dennis Quaid, directed by Lawrence Kasdan

The Earps attempted to do exactly that, but in choosing a poor writer, John Flood, they doomed their project from the outset. A few lines of the unpublished manuscript speak volumes: "Crack! he was in a desperate plight; he felt in front, then at his side, and his hip. Gradually, his hand followed his belt around which had slipped down over one of his hips and he remembered now that in the long ride out, he had loosened his belt to relieve the strain, and the weapon was dangling at his back half way to the ground."

Eventually another writer, Stuart Lake, took over the project, but it was too late. Walter Noble Burns, a hotshot Chicago reporter, essentially wrote a Wyatt Earp book without Earp's help. By the end of 1927, Wyatt's story was on the shelves as *Tombstone: An Iliad of the Southwest*, but he wasn't getting a dime from it.

Only after Wyatt passed away did "his" biography come out. However, Lake, in completing *Wyatt Earp: Frontier Marshal*, falsely attributed many quotes and missed a few key details, such as the location of the gunfight. The confused stories that dogged Wyatt's exploits during his own lifetime would become part of the tapestry of his legend. Lake's account was the model for the early screen adaptations, of which at least five appeared in the 1930s and '40s.

TIN STARS, SILVER SCREEN

Earp! … Wyatt Earp!
Of all frontier peace officers, the best!
Tamed Ellsworth, Wichita, Dodge City, and Tombstone,
Brought law and order to the West.

> —*Earp! A Musical Play in Two Acts,* written by
> Norman J. Fetter, scored by Mark Ollington
> (Earp collection, Arizona Historical Society)

Wyatt Earp, the man, has been far eclipsed by Wyatt Earp, the Myth, whose career spans countless TV shows, novels, films, plays, and at least one musical. While most of the real work in unearthing the true Wyatt has been done by historians, Wyatt the Myth has Hollywood to thank for his fame.

The "Frontier Marshal" inspired no fewer than eleven films made before 1955. But that was only the beginning. A television series, *The Life and Legend of Wyatt Earp,* premiered on September 6, 1955, and became the world's first Western show for grown-ups, running for six years. ABC's Wyatt was a little different from the one we know. As the theme song put it: "The West it was lawless, but one man was flawless, and his is the story you'll hear." The seeds Wyatt had planted in Hollywood finally bore fruit. Two months after the series began, the show's star, Hugh O'Brian, found himself at a dinner function with John Wayne. Wayne told the young man, "I often think of Wyatt Earp when I play a film character. There's a guy who actually did what I'm trying to do." This pure-blinding-white knight's saga stirred interest in the facts behind the Earp legends and generated unreliable new memoirs and articles. "So many old-timers claimed to have witnessed the gunfight in Tombstone that the city council must have put up bleachers along

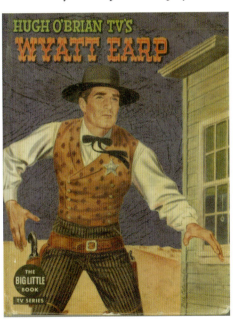

Millions discovered Earp through O'Brian's saintly lawman.

side of the vacant lot and had George Parsons selling popcorn," noted historian Casey Tefertiller. Perhaps inevitably, some scholars set out to debunk Wyatt's glowing reputation. After years of academic battles, it's now safe to say we know Wyatt as a complicated human being, with both flaws and virtues.

The golden age of Earpiana gave way to a revisionist period, with films like the 1967 *Hour of the Gun.* Later, as more of Earp's foibles and true successes came out, the films *Tombstone* (1993) and *Wyatt Earp* (1994) sought to give a more balanced view of the convoluted events in Tombstone.

Throughout it all, Wyatt Earp's story has remained a touchstone for the Wild West. Now, our perceptions of right and wrong in the old days are more nuanced, and Earp stands out not just as a lawman, but as a hopeful man, a proud man, who roamed vast stretches of the West during its tumultuous adolescence. In each retelling of his story, audiences have been captivated by the risk and enterprise of the Old West, and the bravery of those men and women who started new lives in America's frontier boomtowns.

EARPIANA: WHO REMEMBERS WYATT?

Wyatt the man, pacing the courtroom,
long black coat
illuminated by a single star.
Wyatt, the night sky fallen
out of orbit—recounting deeds
to a bony wax day-of-the-dead head ...

—Steve McCabe, *Wyatt Earp in Dallas: 1963*

No doubt the Earp myth will continue to evolve for future generations.

What won't change is the central tenet of Wyatt's fame: the classic story of justice taken outside the law. The Earp saga will always remain a kind of American fairy tale, not so much Disney as the Brothers Grimm. The triumphs and tribulations of real humans are always more appealing than those of perfect beings, and the broad sweep of Wyatt's life and the friendly chaos of Tombstone leave the stage wide open for us to imagine ourselves in the drama. Throngs do it every year, visiting Tombstone, other historic sites, and Western theme parks from Austria to Japan.

What was it really like to sling a gun? My own reenactment took place on a sunny Arizona afternoon, when I donned a Stetson and stood out in a dry arroyo with a well-oiled, century-old Colt .45. You always hear that the gun feels heavier than it looks, but nobody warned me how cool the metal would feel to the touch in the middle of a hot southern Arizona day. Nor did anyone explain how time would stop after I pulled the trigger. The report of the gun seemed to last for a full minute as the barrel kicked up slowly, like a drawbridge in my hands, and the target, an empty plastic jug, did a glacial back-flip twenty yards away. As silence flooded back into the empty riverbed, I could see how justice might become a personal obsession in a world where nearly everyone had the power to stop time at the squeeze of a finger.

These days, playing at the lawman doesn't require an empty riverbed and a stash of bullets. There's a Wyatt Earp card game based on rummy, and, after years of focusing on marauding aliens and World War II, even the video game industry has rediscovered the Old West. Two games released in 2004, *Dead Man's Hand* and *Red Dead Revolver,* allow players the chance to fire their imaginations with shotguns and six-shooters, blasting their way through improbable numbers of outlaws on their own quests for vengeful justice.

The Wyatt Earp legend has also found its way into the fine arts. In 1995, Steve McCabe wrote and illustrated a book-length narrative poem called *Wyatt Earp in Dallas: 1963.* Here Wyatt Earp is seen as an angel of correction, a *deus ex machina* to head off one of the worst shoot-outs of our own time—though the abstract hero of this poem is more ready to buffalo with metaphor than a pistol butt. The poem is a dream of escape: escape from jail, from history, from death.

Seattle-based artist Thom Ross captures the ominous sweep and pathos of the gunfight in his arresting paintings as well as in an illustrated book, *Gunfight at the O.K. Corral.* "This most celebrated event from the Old West is one filled with contradictions," he writes. "It is at once both part of our American myth and history, as well as an unsettled story, in which a swirl of issues and good guys and bad guys continue to perplex us." His images don't always agree with history. Instead, they show us grim-faced heroes and villains in a sort of dream-time Tombstone: "I began using the O.K. Corral in its mythic form as motivation to rise up and confront those obstacles that either frightened or threatened me."

| THE LEGEND OF THE O.K. CORRAL |

‖ TICKET TO ETERNITY ‖

When Wyatt Earp died on January 13, 1929, his last words were "suppose, suppose." He never gave up dreaming. It's for that reason, more than any other, that his story became such a touchstone for America in the decades after his death. He loved the emancipating powers of imagination, whether in tall tales or Shakespeare, and he became a passionate convert to the miracle of celluloid, bridging the gap between the men who took life in both hands and the men who pretended on the silver screen. Wyatt embodied the contradictory ideals of the Old West—stubborn but adaptable, righteous yet ambiguous, lawman and gambler. He was an information man, equally adept at scanning newspapers and saloons. He lived, and died, looking for an angle, but never compromising his integrity.

Wyatt quietly faded away before his story made it to the silver screen.

ABOUT WYATT EARP

Obscured by dust and speculation,
Tombstone straddled legends
like stolen horses. Railroads
nosed at tin stars and silver hills,
lacing down country in steel corsets
and telegraph bustle.

Some men shuddered
to run the future so fast.
They fell, clutching bank notes
and lead medals, gasping up
at gray prospectors' skies,
saluting the dry plane of their last
desert dream through open,
rock-rough palms.

Others lived on, cleaned their guns,
kept reading papers, writing editors,
paring the horizon to make it safe
for tall tales and ice cream gamblers.
Just enough gun smoke, suppose,
in that lonely air, suppose,
to remember by.

—Ed Finn, Tucson, May 2004

SUGGESTED READING

Aleshire, Peter, et al. *Tombstone Chronicles: Tough Folks, Wild Times.* Phoenix, AZ: Arizona Highways Books, 1998.

Ashburn, Frank. *Peabody of Groton.* Cambridge, MA: Riverside Press, 1967.

Jahns, Pat. *Frontier World of Doc Holliday.* Lincoln: University of Nebraska Press, 1998.

The Old West lives on through books, films, and artistic imagination.

Marks, Paula Mitchell. *And Die in the West: The Story of the O.K. Corral Gunfight.* New York: William Morrow, 1989.

Myers, John Myers. *Doc Holliday.* Lincoln: University of Nebraska Press, 1973.

———. *Tombstone's Early Years.* Lincoln: University of Nebraska Press, 1995.

Ross, Thom. *Gunfight at the O.K. Corral.* Golden, CO: Fulcrum Publishing, 2001.

Tefertiller, Casey. *Wyatt Earp: The Life Behind the Legend.* New York: John Wiley, 1997.

Trimble, Marshall. *Arizona: A Cavalcade of History.* Tucson, AZ: Rio Nuevo Publishers, 2003.

Walker, Henry Pickering. "Preacher in Helldorado." *Journal of Arizona History* 15 (1974; this article is also available in pamphlet form at the Episcopal church Peabody helped build in Tombstone).

Waters, Frank. *The Earp Brothers of Tombstone.* Lincoln: University of Nebraska Press, 1960.

ACKNOWLEDGMENTS

I am very grateful to the many people who were so generous with their time and resources as I worked on this book, especially the Deveres of

Tombstone, Terry and Wyatt Earp of Phoenix, Art Austin of the Tombstone Courthouse State Historic Park, Steve and Marge Elliott of the Tombstone Western Heritage Museum, Doug Brown of the Groton School Archives, and the staff of the Arizona Historical Society. Thanks are also due to Thom Ross and Steve McCabe, who kindly allowed me to reproduce their Earp-inspired artistic work. I would especially like to thank the Humphreys family and Rio Nuevo Publishers for suggesting this project and guiding me through it.

PHOTOGRAPHY AND ILLUSTRATION CREDITS AND © AS FOLLOWS:

Mary Humphreys: page 7
W. Ross Humphreys: back cover, pages 1, 3, 4, 5, 16, 19, 21, 22, 62
Thom Ross: front cover illustration
Images on pages 9, 10, and 60 courtesy of the Arizona Historical Society/Tucson, AHS #s 76636, 17483, and 76620, respectively; used with permission.